1 MONTH OF FREE READING

at

www.ForgottenBooks.com

By purchasing this book you are eligible for one month membership to ForgottenBooks.com, giving you unlimited access to our entire collection of over 1,000,000 titles via our web site and mobile apps.

To claim your free month visit:

www.forgottenbooks.com/free1374842

ISBN 978-1-397-31558-8
PIBN 11374842

This book is a reproduction of an important historical work. Forgotten Books uses state-of-the-art technology to digitally reconstruct the work, preserving the original format whilst repairing imperfections present in the aged copy. In rare cases, an imperfection in the original, such as a blemish or missing page, may be replicated in our edition. We do, however, repair the vast majority of imperfections successfully; any imperfections that remain are intentionally left to preserve the state of such historical works.

TRY AND ARBORICULTURE

IN

MASSACHUSETTS.

By PROF. JOHN ROBINSON.

A paper read before the winter meeting of the assachusetts Board of Agriculture at Springfield, Decnber 6, 1887, and printed with the thirty-fifth annual port of the Board, 1887.

FORESTRY AND ARBORICULTURE

IN MASSACHUSETTS.

BY PROF. JOHN ROBINSON OF SALEM.

Ladies and Gentlemen, — It has been concisely stated in the report of a forest commission of a neighboring State that " a wise economy in the use of the natural resources of a country should recognize the fact that certain regions of the earth's surface are adapted by nature to remain covered with forests, and that any attempt to devote such regions to other purposes can only be followed by failure and disaster." *

Through the work on the forests of the United States, published in connection with the census of 1880,† it is now possible to form a correct estimate of the immense economic value of our forests. In this volume full accounts are given of the four hundred trees which make up our forest flora, and nearly every one is shown to possess some special value or adaptation to special surroundings.

A knowledge, too, of the physical importance of the forests, as shown by a careful study of the effect produced by their removal, both in this country and in Europe, is becoming widely disseminated.

With the destruction of the forests the springs disappear and the flow of water in the rivers is often so much reduced in summer that navigation is suspended and machinery stopped, while in the spring the rains and melted snows pour down in destructive torrents the waters which the for-

---

* Report For. Commis. State N. Y. 1885, p. 5.
† Forest Trees of N. A., Rep. U. S. Census, 1880, Vol. IX.

mer forests in a great measure held back for gradual distri-
bution throughout the season. Storms of wind and pelting
hail sweep resistlessly over the bared lands, the fury of
which was checked, or entirely abated, by the tall forests of
the past. Our seasons are considered hotter in summer
and colder in winter than formerly, and the frosts reach
deeper into the soil and remain there longer in the
spring.*

It would be difficult to determine just what percentage of
the land should remain covered with forest growth in order
to meet all the requirements of man, and at the same time
preserve a proper climatic balance. According to the soil
and atmospheric conditions of the locality, its distance
from the ocean and the direction of prevailing winds, a
variation of from ten to thirty-five per cent. of forest
cover may be given as some indication of the proportion
required.†

Here in Massachusetts, one of the most important services
which can be rendered by the forest trees is that of binding
together and retaining in place the shifting sands which
cover such large areas of our sea coast. In many cases a
thoughtless destruction of the trees which formerly grew
near the shore has allowed the encroaching sands to over-
whelm territory once under cultivation. In one familiar
instance an apple orchard at Ipswich lies, buried to
the upper branches of the trees in a mass of fine white
sand.

It is gratifying to know, however, although we have suf-
fered by this destruction of trees on our exposed coast, that
one of the very few examples of the ability to successfully
replant these waste shore lands, and at a comparatively
small cost, is to be found in the plantation of pitch pine in
the south-eastern portion of our State. Of these it has
justly been said : — " The real progress in sylviculture in
Massachusetts has been made by the farmers of Barnstable
and Plymouth counties, who have taught us how to plant
and raise forests successfully and profitably, under the most

* " The Earth as Modified by Human Action." G. P. Marsh, chap. III., pp. 148
to 397.

† *Ibid.*, also Fernow, Report Forestry Bureau. 1886, p. 153, note.

unfavorable conditions." *   The cause of their success is that they took their lessons from nature and not from foreign books, and used for their plantations the trees natural to the soil.

Owing to the nature of our American institutions we have in this country a much more difficult problem to solve, in determining the methods by which to preserve existing forests and to replant those already destroyed, than is encountered in Europe, where public opinion is already educated to comprehend the necessity of stringent forest laws.   To quote again the report first referred to :† — " A forest law to effect its purpose must rest on a broad and solid basis of public interest.   The only real safety for the forest will be found in the appreciation of its value by the community."

The terrible destruction of the forests in this country, pursued of late years in the most wickedly wasteful manner, combined with the forest fires, but little restricted as yet (and which annually destroy more timber than is used for all mechanical purposes together), if continued, will transform into deserts some of the most beautiful and valuable territory in the United States, and convert lands which might be perpetually covered with timber into woodless, uninhabitable barrens.

It has been estimated that the immense consumption of white pine, together with the wasteful methods practised in cutting it, will entirely exhaust the marketable supply in the three great pine-producing states of Michigan, Wisconsin and Minnesota in " a comparatively short time."‡   And even if the vast resources of the South be added, and all the woods capable of being used interchangeably with pine be summed together, it will take but fifty years,§ at even the present rate of consumption, to produce a similar effect in the whole United States.   This has led speculators to purchase large areas of Western and Southern forests.

* Some additional notes on tree planting. C. S. Sargent, Rep. State Bd. Ag. Mass. 1885, p. 377.

† Report Forest Commis. State N. Y., 1885, p. 28.

‡ Report U. S. Census 1880, Vol. IX., p. 490. " Twelve or fifteen years " is given as an estimate of the time by the N. Y. Nation, Feb. 16, 1882.

§ See Rep. U. S. Ag. Div. Forestry, B. E. Fernow, 1886, p. 157.

It is stated in the last report of the forestry division at Washington, by Mr. B. E. Fernow,* that the Bavarian government recently sent an expert to this country to examine into our forest resources and the demands made upon them, with the view of profiting by our miserable plight. Upon being questioned as to his mission this agent answered : — " In fifty years you will have to import your timber, and as you will probably have a preference for American kinds, we shall now begin to grow them in order to be ready to send them to you at the proper time."

It may not be possible for a German State to grow timber for the American market in fifty years, but the statement shows, however, the superiority of German over American methods in forest management. It also shows that an expert from a country where forest questions are fully understood agrees with American writers in estimating the time we shall take to destroy the lumber-producing forests of the West.

Our special interest is of course centered in the effects of the removal of the forests in our own State and the necessities for reforestation and the extent to which it should be carried on here. We are, according to the way we look at the matter, in a fortunate or an unfortunate position in Massachusetts.

The geographical position of New England, coming as it does within the influence of the moisture-laden, ocean breezes, assures for us a sufficient and evenly distributed rainfall, and makes the forest of less climatic importance than in the interior of the continent.

Therefore, although the data and the startling conclusions to be drawn from them, in relation to the calamities which must inevitably follow the destruction of the forests, are all important, and as patriotic citizens we should seek to avert those dangers which threaten, through forest destruction, our national prosperity, still, here in Massachusetts, the destruction of the forests outside of New England, however improvidently it may be pursued, will never in any probability injuriously affect our climate, water supply, or gen-

* See Rep. U. S. Ag. Div. Forestry, B. E. Fernow, 1886, p. 155, note.

eral health. In fact, it is quite possible, if the present methods of lumbering are persisted in, that the price of timber will advance sufficiently to enable our people to engage in forest culture on quite a large scale.

Our original forests were long ago cut, but owing to the decline of some other agricultural pursuits and the growing interest in forest culture, the woods throughout the State are likely to increase rather than diminish in quantity and to occupy many of our pastures and present bare and rocky hillsides. It therefore becomes important for us to care for our growing forests, and by judiciously selecting species and properly planting new ones, be prepared to have what timber we can to sell to our friends and neighbors when the fifty years' supply now standing in the American forests is exhausted. In the position we hold in this respect we may be considered as fortunate, or, at least, there need be no danger of meeting with misfortune.

Taken by itself, however, Massachusetts is in one way unfortunately situated, for the reason that the two great rivers of importance in connection with our manufacturing interests, the Connecticut and Merrimac, both take their rise a long distance to the north of us in New Hampshire. Any attempt, therefore, to control the flow of their waters by systems looking to a retention of a forest growth on the mountain slopes at their sources is absolutely impossible, as far as the power of Massachusetts to do so is concerned.

The same may be said of some of the smaller rivers which furnish water power to mills in other portions of the State. In fact, the only streams at whose sources the State could by any means within itself regulate the cutting of the forests or replant denuded hillsides are some of the smaller tributaries of the Connecticut and the Housatonic.

As this state of things has long existed here, many manufacturing corporations have supplemented their water power with steam, or have provided themselves with reservoirs which control in a more or less satisfactory degree the flow of the water in the streams upon which their business depends. Thus, at great expense, provisions have been made to take the place of the forests, the natural regulators of the rivers, although, even with these safeguards, a system of protective forest management is of the utmost importance at the sources of our two great rivers in New Hampshire.

In 1883 a commission was appointed in New Hampshire to inquire into the condition of the forests of that State and report what action might be advisable for their protection. The report, which was printed in 1885, is of much interest to us in Massachusetts, for it is encouraging to know that, aside from the effects of forest destruction in New Hampshire alone, it considers the effect of such destruction on the rivers upon which so many manufacturing towns in Massachusetts are situated. There is also much information of practical value to be gathered from this report in relation to methods of re-forestation and the selection of species to use, which, owing to the similarity of soil and climate, are as applicable to the Massachusetts as the New Hampshire plantations.

These suggestions naturally point to the importance of co-operation in matters of forestry. We are as a country admirably situated to control our forest affairs for the protection of our rivers, and to prevent, as far as it is possible to do so, undesirable changes of climate and injurious mechanical influences.

Except, however, in a few instances like that of New York, which contains within its own borders the sources of its most important stream, the individual States, cut out regardless of natural divisions, are without power to establish any system of forest management which will be of the slightest benefit to themselves or protective of the industries carried on by their citizens. On the other hand, it may be possible for a single State, by a bad forest policy, or by no policy at all, to injure or even ruin the property in a neighboring State, while having no vital interests of its own to suffer.

It is hardly to be expected that legislatures will be so bound by the golden rule as to enact laws for the protection of their neighbors when they are as yet too often indifferent to the importance of such action to protect the interests of their own citizens, and hence we are forced to the conclusion, that to be effective and just for all, our forest policy must be a national one. Such a policy should be paternal in its nature, and yet leave in the hands of the individual States the power to regulate forest matters not inconsistent with the welfare of the country as a whole.

We Americans do not like to be hedged about with legal restrictions. The land in a great measure, especially in the older States, is in the hands of the farmers. Outside of New York but very little of it is in the hands of the State governments. It therefore becomes evident that the people must be educated to their necessity, before sufficient and satisfactory laws can be enacted and carried out to protect and preserve our existing forests, or to reforest regions already stripped of their cover.

The forests of this country are its most valuable property. They are perhaps the most important as they are the most accessible forests in the world. They are of the utmost value physically and commercially, and their destruction is imminent. We have no forest policy, no school of forestry, and but few educated forest experts to look to for advice or to direct a forest policy, provided one is ever adopted. What then is to be done? We must have a national forest policy and establish a national forest school.

Much has been said and written of late in relation to forest schools and instruction in forestry in our colleges and agricultural institutes. As far as this may serve to give the student a general knowledge of the underlying principles of the subject, and through him diffuse a sense of the importance of governmental action and the reasons therefor, it is well and good that such instruction should be given. With a majority of students, however, the time devoted to their college work is so short, and their desire for other courses of study is so great, that any attempt to produce skilled foresters by the system now in vogue, or with the present available corps of instructors in any of our colleges, or in connection with other courses of study, must inevitably result in miserable failure.

One very important factor in connection with the study of forestry is too often overlooked. Taking it for granted that it is possible to produce an expert forester in this country by a course of study in any of our institutions of learning, or that a fully equipped forest school should be established,

the man who desires to become a forester will naturally ask
the question, " What employment can I obtain when my
education is completed to warrant this great outlay of time
and money?" And under the present condition of things
the answer must be, " There is none."

A nurseryman may find employment, or a landscape
gardener, even, to take charge of some public park or private plantation ; but there is not now in this country a single
opening for a trained forester. Therefore, until some occu-
pation is guaranteed, there can be no students of forestry,
for the demand must first come in this case to create the
supply.

It is absolutely necessary that the establishment of a forest
school should be preceded by the adoption of a national
policy of forest protection and by the appointment of forest
commissioners, forest inspectors or a forest guard ; for, until
it has been irrevocably determined to preserve and maintain
public forests, the forest school would be useless and no
student would join it on account of the uncertainty of future
legislation.

The policy being determined upon, it would have to be
carried out for the first ten or fifteen years by comparatively
inexperienced persons, but, eventually, students trained in
the school would be available for administrative positions.

Private forest schools, however munificently endowed,
would bear the same relation to a national school that the
private military academies, which have sprung up throughout the United States, do to the West Point Academy.
Their graduates would not be sure of Government employment and there is no one but the Government, now at least,
to employ foresters.

The forest school should be conducted on precisely the
same principles as the United States Military Academy.
Students should be accepted on a competitive examination
and receive pay or allowance from the Government as provided for the West Point cadets at the present time. The
course of study should extend for a term of five to eight
years and the students be given, when graduated, a permanent appointment in the forest service, with opportunity
for promotion. In this way and in no other may we expect

students to attend a school of forestry, if one should be established, or can we ever have a forest policy or a system of forest protection and preservation worthy of the name.

If the first work of the Government was merely the establishment of a forest guard, and nothing more be accomplished than to partially restrict the forest fires which are now so destructive, it is certain that an amount of timber would annually be saved much exceeding in value the cost of such service.

Even here in Massachusetts, notwithstanding the comparatively small size of the trees and the isolation of the forests themselves, and in the face of the penalties affixed for setting forest fires, there was destroyed in 1880 alone wood to the value of upwards of one hundred thousand dollars, — covering fourteen thousand acres of land.* This fear of fire discourages investments in woodlands and sends capital, which naturally would be used for this purpose, in other directions in search of greater security.

The injury done to woodlands by browsing animals, by exterminating seedling trees, and barking those of larger growth, is, on the whole, as great, and in many cases greater, than that done by fires. Browsing domestic animals not only injure the woodlands directly, but they prevent a future growth by eating the seeds as well as the young trees.

The preference shown by hogs for the sweet fruit of the white oak, beech and chestnut is causing these species to become replaced in our forests by less valuable but bitter fruited trees. In California, too, the sheep are endangering the life and perpetuation of some of the finest forests in the world.† The unscientific methods of farming which permit this practice are to be condemned and should be corrected at once.

It would be a wiser economy for us in Massachusetts to provide pasturage for browsing animals by a higher cultivation of the land, so that the largest number could be pastured on the fewest acres. It is certainly a bad policy which obliges cattle to travel all day for a miserable subsistence.

* Forests of N. A. Rep. U. S. Census, 1880, Vol. IX., p. 500.
† *Ibid.*, p. 492. See also " The Earth as Modified by Human Action," G. P. Marsh, p. 382.

The land which is naturally adapted for a forest growth is not suitable for pasturage; and inversely, the land which is suitable for pasturage is too valuable to be given up to forests.

The economic value of the forests of Massachusetts may be summed up in a few words, — enough, however, to show the importance of fostering care to preserve our present forest growth and of encouraging its increase. The value of the wood used for fuel in Massachusetts reached, in 1880, a sum of upwards of four million six hundred thousand dollars; and, aside from this, capital to the amount of two and one-half millions of dollars is invested in lumber manufacturing in this State, in which business thirty-one hundred hands are at times engaged, to whom nearly half a million dollars are annually paid for wages.*

This is in a State which is hardly considered in making up the lumber statistics of the country; and yet we have at Winchendon some of the most important wooden-ware man-ufacturing establishments in the world.† We must feel, therefore (small as we appear on the map, and insignificant as is our position in the list of lumber-producing States), that we have industries in wood by no means to be despised, and which, owing to the favorable condition of the climate and soil for the production of certain useful woods, and the changes taking place in the uses of land for agricultural purposes, may be profitably encouraged and greatly devel-oped.

The only forest planting, however, likely to become general here must be upon a small scale. For such planta-tions no tree is so well adapted both to soil and climate, or so free from destruction by drought, disease or the attack of insects, as the white pine. It is readily obtained, easily cultivated, and is more certain to bring profitable returns,— and that too in a shorter time, — than almost any other species. For drier soil and upon the sandy coast the red pine or the pitch pine may, of course, be substituted, with a success proved by actual experiment.

Profitable plantations of European larch have also been

* Forests of N. A. Rep. U. S. Census, 1880, Vol. IX., p. 486.
† Ibid., p. 501. "The most important point in the United States."

made here; and the Douglas fir, to which attention was called in a previous paper* (in a small plantation in the eastern part of the State†), has shown promise of rivalling some of the native conifers by its strong growth; but the seeds and young plants of this species must of course be of Colorado stock to succeed in this climate.

Of the deciduous trees, the hickory, ash, chestnut and rock maple are the most desirable for us. They furnish a sufficient variety of this class and are sure to produce timber of marketable value. To reduce this list still further, the farmers of Massachusetts are safe if they centre all their efforts on the white pine, ash, hickory and chestnut.

The ash thrives here in perfection, and as its wood must always be in demand for tool handles, for which purpose alone immense quantities are annually used, it is a most important and valuable tree for our plantations.

The hickory, also used for tool handles and wagon wheels, is no less important, and as good hickory wood, like ash, is growing scarcer every year, it should be planted whenever possible.

The chestnut is a tree of rapid growth and is, for various reasons, the most desirable species to plant here for the production of fence posts and railroad ties. To be sure, these trees require good soil, but they could be planted by the roadsides and along division walls and fences much more than at present.

Too much cannot be said to urge our farmers to plant each year some hickory nuts or chestnuts, or to care for the natural seedlings of these trees. This is the simplest form of forest tree culture, the easiest and the least expensive. It would occupy but little time, and if generally pursued the value of the farms of Massachusetts would be immensely increased.

By enclosing any young natural plantations, protecting them from fire and from browsing animals, and weeding out worthless over-topping trees, a sure profit may be obtained from thousands of acres of land in Massachusetts now practically of no value.

---

* Ornamental Trees for Mass. Plant. Rep. St. Bd. Ag. 1880, p. 23.
† Estate of Mrs. John C. Phillips, N. Beverly, near Wenham Lake.

Many accounts have been published, substantiated by figures, of the profits of tree planting in New England, and even if we allow an enormous margin for accident and occasioual failure, an average result of fair profit is most certainly assured, larger in proportion than can be shown for most agricultural crops where the original outlay is no greater.

A recent editorial in one of our leading daily journals* on "abandoned farms" in Massachusetts, gives a gloomy picture of the deserted fields and rapidly decaying houses of the once well-kept and profitable farms, and asks the question, Why is this so? The answer given, is : first, because the expense of fertilizing is so great ; second, that less labor in other directions will bring larger profits ; and third, man's instinctive dislike to isolation.

The ease, cheapness and rapidity with which all produce can now be delivered at our doors, even from places as far off as California and the tropical islands to the south of us, have brought the fruit and vegetables from these distant regions in direct competition with the earliest forced products of the farm and market garden. This, together with other causes, has made a great change in farm practice in New England, and renders it imperative that means should be devised to meet this competition, and also to find the best ways of utilizing these deserted farm lands ; although it should have been stated that no really good farming lands have ever been deserted.

The article referred to suggests one remedy in the theory of "ten acres enough," and says : "If would-be farmers would content themselves with ground which they and their children could cultivate unaided, and devote themselves to selected products, there would be less disappointment and fewer failures among the farmers of New England." But strangely enough, nothing is said in relation to planting these worn-out and deserted farms to forests, although a hint is thrown out in this direction when reference is made to "trees which have grown up in the fields formerly plowed and sowed, so that the owner is already counting their value at some lone saw mill."

* Boston Daily Advertiser, Nov. 2, 1887

These very lands, however, which nature never intended should be farmed, might be wisely and profitably planted with white pine, and as the taxes in that case would be remitted under our laws, and hence be no further burden in that respect for ten years, the owner, while following the advice previously given as to small farms and selected products, could at the same time be making an investment which would at least insure profit to his children.

So many sources are available for obtaining information in regard to tree planting, the proper varieties to select for certain soils, methods of cultivation, thinning and pruning, it is not necessary to speak of these matters here in a merely general way. It is certain, however, that a studious man of ordinary intelligence and tact will bring about better results for himself than any hard and fast rules, laid down in books, can do for him. It is to the practical application of lessons taught us by observing our natural forests, and the results of patiently conducted experiments, that we may look for the exact rules which will govern the work of the future planter, and which, inasmuch as this subject is for us a new one, we must find out for ourselves. To use the words of a recent writer :* — " As in the medicine the charlatan will prescribe without diagnosis, so in forestry he must be called a charlatan who would attempt to give rules applicable to all conditions and under all circumstances. A diagnosis not only of the local conditions as to soil, climate and flora, but also of the objects and financial capacity of the would-be forester, must precede special advice."

Aside from the question of forests and their relation to commerce in forest products, which pertain comparatively to a few, there is very much to be gained here by the encouragement of roadside and ornamental tree planting. This should not be lost sight of for a moment, as in this nearly every one of us may participate.

Any observing person, during the last twenty-five years, must have noticed the rapid and gratifying increase in yard and window gardening in almost every village and town. Not only in quantity but in their quality, too, a marked improvement is to be seen in the plants grown. This prac-

* Rep. Forestry Div. Dep. Ag. Washington, 1886, B. E. Fernow, p. 223.

tice is already ·being extended to the cultivation of attractive
trees and shrubs, and it only requires the encouragement of
good examples to develop it to a far greater degree.

Good opportunity, too, is offered in our rural cemeteries
for planting a great variety of ornamental trees. There is
no place where they could be grown more appropriately;
and yet there are but few cemeteries in our country towns
where much if any attention is paid to this matter, and in
some cases they are positively repulsive in appearance.

Vast improvements have been made in the cemeteries in
the vicinity of cities during the last fifty years, but most of
the others are as yet nothing more than modern graveyards,
which do not even possess the quiet attractiveness of those
of the earlier colonial period where, without the preten-
tiousness of modern " monuments," the inconspicuous slate
head stones, scattered among the trees, harmonize with the
scene. There is room for much good work in this direction
by the village improvement associations.

·· The new industry," as the increase of summer visitors
to the shore and country is now called, has a considerable
influence on the cultivation of ornamental trees throughout
the State. Those who establish summer homes on the sea
shore, or in the rural districts, are favorably disposed to the
trees; and indeed, the value of many estates for this purpose is in a great measure dependent on the condition and
position of the trees upon them.

It is to this class of residents and their influence that we
are indebted for the greater beauty and healthfulness of
many towns. This work of beautifying country homes is
being so far extended, that some of our older villages in the
western part of the State are being transformed into charm-
ing parks and will in time vie with the much praised country-
side of Old England.

In a paper read before this board in 1880,* the subject of
suitable trees for ornamental plantations was fully considered
as based upon the study of the climatic conditions under
which the trees best thrive. The conclusions drawn were
that, for New England (with few exceptions), New England
trees are the best; that many additional species may be

---

* Ornamental Trees for Mass. Plant. Rep. St. Bd. Ag. 1880, p. 23.

taken from the forests of the middle States and Alleghany Mountains and a few from the Rocky Mountain region, and also that the exotic species used should come from eastern Asia rather than western Europe.

There are many matters to be especially considered in making an ornamental plantation, and still others in selecting trees for the streets and roadsides. Trees naturally grow massed together, and, therefore, when one is planted in an isolated position it will be exposed to very different influences than when surrounded by its fellows in the forest. The additional exposure to the wind and to the sunlight, which reaches even to its lower branches, has the effect of encouraging a more spreading growth with a decrease in height. Single trees, too, are inclined to fruit more freely, especially the conifers which, under certain conditions, over-bear to such an extent as to check their development, thus exhausting the trees and shortening their period of growth and beauty.

For these reasons it may be found that certain native trees which attain perfection here in a forest will not withstand the exposure if planted in the field or by the roadside, while others (including some foreign species which are not to be recommended for ornamental purposes), may prove suitable for forest planting.

The evergreens should, if possible, be grown in a light soil, with a richer upper soil, for a tree will flourish in such a situation, while in a cold, heavy soil it will make a late start and a slow growth that will be overtaken by the autumn frosts before opportunity has been given for the ripening of the new wood. The trouble arising from such soil, however, may sometimes be overcome by under draining.

For our city streets there are comparatively few suitable trees from which to make selection, for many species which are desirable for plantations and ornamental purposes in parks and lawns, and for roadsides in the rural districts, do not meet the requirements of the city.

The tree most frequently planted now is the rock maple, which is well enough when used in reasonable numbers and when planted in suitable places, but it should not, as is too often the case, be used to the exclusion of all other species.

For a wide street there is no tree that can equal the American elm in producing the arched effect so much admired in many of our older towns, but the elm requires a good soil and is impatient of drought, and should not, therefore, be planted in dry, poor land. The desire for immediate effect ought not to cause this tree to be cast aside in places where it is possible for it to flourish, of which there appears to be a great danger, for the beautiful streets of arching elms which have made the towns of the Connecticut Valley so famous should never be allowed to become merely traditional, for here this tree grows in its utmost luxuriance.

In the more crowded streets of the cities, however, the European elm, a tree of naturally wide range, has proved more satisfactory. For more than one hundred years this tree has been grown in New England. Its habit is more dense and it retains its foliage much longer in the autumn than the American tree. It better endures the poorer atmosphere of the city, and it is free from the attacks of the canker-worm, which so often disfigure the American elm. It is, therefore, a much better tree for our city streets than the native elm, and one which may be considered as fairly tested here by actual experiment.

In the vicinity of the sea shore the Norway maple is a most desirable tree, but in the interior its leaves often become rusty as the season advances, making it less suitable for such situations than the native rock maple. The white maple, too, is a tree of most graceful habit, but it is best seen when planted in parks or lawns, although it answers well for the less frequented streets. The white ash may also be used in some cases with good effect, and the bass wood, red maple and Dutch elm, are of value in proper situations. The red oak has proved in many places a fine street tree, growing in one instance faster than the rock maple, and for many streets in the country towns the hickory, birch, chestnut, necklace poplar and some other species may be used which would not be suitable for city streets.

The selection and planting of trees for our streets should always be placed in the hands of some general committee or permanent board. If left to the abutter, a scattered, irregular collection of all sorts of trees — good, bad and indif-ferent — will be the result ; whereas, in the hands of a properly constituted body, the streets can be planted uniformly with the sort of trees best adapted to the particular situation and desirably varied as the work proceeds in different local-ities.

Tearing up trees from the swamp or hillsides, stripping them to bare poles and squarely cutting of their tops, so commonly practised in planting the maple and some other species, cannot be too severely condemned. The trees thus treated may at first put out luxuriant heads, and for a time appear to do well, but, as the branches fork at the place where the top was cut off, a large exposed space is left in which water collects, rotting the centre of the tree and sooner or later causing deformity or death. This is the principal reason why so many maple trees of a certain age are failing all over New England.

It would be much better to plant nursery grown trees in our streets. We are far behind the rest of the world in this respect. In Germany and France, and even in Japan, trees are selected and planted with the utmost care. There is no reason why our cities and towns and perhaps the local improvement associations should not establish nurseries for the special purpose of producing suitable trees for streets and roadside planting.

In the streets of many of the cities and larger towns the old trees, which in many cases seem to have been planted with great care and good judgment, are now disappearing through loss by old age, the march of improvement and the demands of commerce. In such streets as are devoted to business purposes, often too narrow already, it is not to be expected that trees will ever be planted. There are, how-ever, entire streets, with either decrepit and miserable apolo-gies for shade trees, or often none at all, where there is abundant room to plant them, and where they would greatly improve the appearance of the street, as well as add comfort to all persons frequenting it. But even if the abutter or the local improvement society, or even the town or city authori-ties themselves, plant street trees, there are many vexing obstacles to the accomplishment of the best results.

Those in charge of the laying of drains or the setting of edgestones do not think for a moment of arranging their work to avoid a tree, but instead, roots and buttresses are cut and slashed without mercy. Horses are tied to young trees and old by the hour together, and many a succulent luncheon is made from the bark and nascent wood. Trees are often seen in city streets where a few feet from the ground only a small portion of the circumference of the bark is left, and many fine shade trees are annually destroyed from this cause.

Another source of great loss of trees in cities arises from the leaks into the earth in which they live from poorly and improperly laid gas mains. In some cities, to avoid interference with the systems of sewer and water pipes, the gas mains are placed so near the surface that every winter they are thrown and broken by the frost. In one instance, twenty distinct gas leaks were found in the mains of a single street, not one quarter of a mile in length, in one of the cities of our eastern seaboard. When thoroughly permeated with the gas, the earth retains it for years, and tree after tree may be planted; and even if a large amount of fresh earth be added each time, the trees will fail to live. Trees in streets and parks, it is stated, have been killed by having the land about their trunks filled to a depth of two or three feet, thus showing that trees, no more than animals, will endure being buried alive.

In roadside tree planting, even in the rural districts where many of the obstacles met with in the cities are avoided, it is impossible to produce the best results unless the roads are properly laid out, and, together with the roadsides, are well cared for.

Many country roads are made unnecessarily wide at the outset. It is not uncommon to see a poorly built, poorly kept, broad expanse of gravel, wider than many of the most crowded thorougfares of the city, where the travel is confined to one or two cart tracks meandering through its weary length.

A narrower roadway could be maintained in better condition at less cost, and, if it was desirable to retain a greater width for future use, by allowing the grass and bushes to grow at the sides, a minimum of gravelly surface would be exposed to the winds, and much of the nuisance arising from the great clouds of dust be avoided through the dry season.

The desirability of good and attractive roads for ordinary travel, as well as for pleasure driving, must be admitted. Here, too, the formal effect of regularly planted street trees should give place to a more natural grouping, with a greater variety of species, and a judicious growth of bushes, herbs and climbing plants should be encouraged at the roadside and along the walls and fences.

Where such already exist, the shrubs and other plants are frequently cut down and left in rough piles, thus transforming into a rubbish heap that which was before an interesting garden bed. For what reason this is done, or why, as is too often the case, the little gullies at the roadside are allowed to be filled up with refuse from the shoemaker's shop or with tin cans and other discarded household effects, it is difficult to imagine.

Another pernicious custom, in vogue in the vicinity of Boston, is to burn at the roadside the leaves and brush collected during the spring and autumn clearings of the road. These fires, of course, disfigure a certain space each time and in many instances spread into the surrounding bushes, injuring the appearance of the roadside and endangering the life of any trees which may be growing there by burning the bark about their trunks.

As the care of the country roads is usually subdivided among the farmers of the town, no special system is adopted, and a variety of treatment is given the roadside as well as the roads themselves. A systematic management in the hands of one competent man has been shown, where it has been tried,* to give much better results, without additional expense.

To quote a little volume recently published as a law book : † "Good roads have a tendency to make the country a desirable dwelling-place, and a town which is noted for its good roads becomes the abode of people of taste, wealth and intelligence." There is law enough to protect the road-

* Town of Chelmsford, Mass., 66. "The Road and the Roadside," Potter, p. 25.
† *Ibid.*, p. 10.

side and shade trees, but the lack is in the public sentiment to enforce it.

These matters are of interest to the roadside tree planter, for the condition of the roads, the shrubs at their margins, and the neatness of the walls and fences, all contribute to the general effect, and must receive the attention they deserve, if we are to take the trouble to plant trees at all, or desire to make our country-side what it should be.

There is no royal road to success in tree planting, and the ultimate accomplishment of good results must often be reached through many disappointments and discouragements. The trees are frequently attacked by mysterious fungi on their leaves and at their roots and insect enemies innumerable are to be encountered, to a far greater extent in ornamental plantations than in the thicker growth of the forest. Every locality has its peculiar surroundings, — currents of wind, conditions and quality of the soil, and, in ornamental plantations, associated scenery and buildings. These must all be carefully considered before accepting the advice of the essayist, who can only lay down general rules and give general lists of trees from which the planter must make selection for special cases.

A great mistake is often made, in attempting to get quick results, by planting trees of too great size. Smaller nursery-grown trees, if well chosen and properly planted, will always prove the best and soon outstrip the larger ones set out at the same time. It is well in tree planting to " make haste slowly."

The observation of Arbor Day, which originated in Nebraska in 1874, has gradually extended to other States, until it has now become a generally established institution. To be sure, the lists of exercises which are published for use on the occasions of its celebration are poetic and sentimental rather than practical, yet if, as suggested in the last report of the United States Forestry Bureau, Arbor Day and its observation really offers a means " for getting the facts relating to tree growth and the practical uses of trees before the minds of the old and young alike, and for creating and diffusing throughout the community a sentiment which promises much good to the cause of forestry," it is an invention not without some value.

It may possibly be necessary, in order to call the attention of busy people to this subject, to set apart a special day for tree planting and to make it a public holiday; but it would be much better if these matters could be kept in mind every day, and the children in our schools, and the older people as well, could become more generally informed as to the necessity for forests and their importance in political and domestic economy, and more familiar with the trees met with in every day life, rather than by condensing all their efforts into one day of poetical effusion and song.

That such knowledge is sadly needed is evidenced by daily illustrations. To give one example : — A class in an advanced school desiring to celebrate the centennial anniversary of our independence of British authority, planted a tree on the school grounds; but, not being familiar with these matters, they took without question what a dealer sent them, and celebrated the event by planting an English oak, an emblem of royalty, and naturally a poor tree in this climate, which may now be seen starved and puny, and looking as if it fully appreciated the inappropriateness of its selection.

Although there seems to be a very general interest shown in the forests and in the cultivation of ornamental trees, there are, however, but few persons who are sufficiently familiar with our native trees to call them by name. There are of course many who can tell an elm from an oak, or a willow from a pine, but there are not many who can name the different species of oak or pine, or even distinguish the pines from the spruces, — who can see the difference between birches and hornbeams, or separate the many foreign trees in cultivation from the native species. In fact, the native trees and the grasses and sedges, by far the most conspicuous plants in our flora and forming its greater bulk, are the ones least known and the least studied by the people.

The trees are neither numerous in species, nor is there any difficulty whatever in distinguishing one from another among those of native growth, and it certainly seems that the pleasure and satisfaction of their intimate acquaintance would be a sufficient inducement to reward any one for the time expended in studying them.

For the purpose of aiding a class which met last spring at the rooms of the Peabody Academy of Science for botanical study, a list of trees and tree-like shrubs was prepared, including such species, native and introduced, of which good growing specimens could be seen in the immediate vicinity of Salem, and to show how few species it was necessary to know in order to become familiar with the trees in one's neighborhood.

This list included but 113 species, of which 64 were natives of eastern Massachusetts, 17 were introduced from other portions of the United States, and 32 came from foreign countries.

If to this list a dozen less common trees be added, making the total number 125, it will cover all the species that are required to be known in order to name, at sight, every tree met with in our walks in the woods, along country roads or in the city streets and parks of this State, outside of a botanical garden or the collection of some enthusiastic arboriculturist. It does not seem, therefore, that the task of becoming acquainted with them presents great difficulties or is likely to exhaust much time to master it.

Classes or clubs for the study of native trees and so much of structural botany as might be applicable to them, or the introduction of such study into clubs and classes already formed, would be the means of bringing a knowledge of these matters to our young people in a very pleasant way. It would at the same time offer a rational excuse for social meetings in many places where public exhibitions and lectures are infrequent.

There is, without doubt, in every town, some one sufficiently familiar with the subject to act as a leader for a class in tree study; and a small assessment in a class of twenty persons would purchase all the available books required for reference. Of course, it would be desirable that as much of the work as possible should be done during the summer months; but as it would probably be more convenient to meet on winter evenings, specimens could be collected the previous summer for winter use.

The knowledge acquired in this way, practically applied afterward in going about the country in ordinary pursuits, would soon familiarize the student with the trees and add much pleasure to daily walks and drives.

The interest which would undoubtedly be developed could not fail to lead, in many cases, to further study and a more general diffusion of practical information in regard to trees and kindred subjects. The formation of such classes is to be commended in every way and might profitably supplant the clubs, now so fashionable, formed to struggle with the intricacies of Browning and Shelley. For however desirable it may be to become acquainted with profound writers, there is a morbid tendency just now in these literary matters not well to encourage. Any study, therefore, which takes one out of doors, and with all things fresh and healthful, can be cheerfully recommended. To study the trees is as good for the body as the mind. Through walks and drives our system is invigorated and the blood is sent coursing more freshly through our veins, while a fund of valuable and practical information is being gained at the same time.

The study of trees, both in their botanical and economic aspects, — the establishment of ornamental plantations, or tree planting in the street or by the roadside, as well as the care or the creation of more extensive forest reserves, — all tend to the good of the Commonwealth and the prosperity of its citizens. It is fitting, therefore, to close this essay with the words of one who unceasingly felt the deepest interest in these subjects; and although only remembered personally by the passing generation has left us, in his volume on the "Trees and Shrubs of Massachusetts," a work which will ever cause him to be held in grateful esteem.

In the closing paragraph of a chapter on the physical and economic importance of the forests to our State, and which wears well the forty years it has been written, Mr. Emerson says* : —

But why should it be thought important to reclaim or render valuable the waste or worthless lands of Massachusetts? There are millions of acres in the western States far richer than

* Emerson. "Trees and Shrubs of Mass.," 1846, p. 36. 2d. ed, 1875, p. 43.

any in our State. Why not go thither and occupy the rich, wild lands? There are various reasons. Every improvement in agriculture, in the management of the forests, and in the use of the other natural resources of our State, makes it capable of sustaining a larger population and thus enabling more of our young men and women to remain with us. The advantages of our life in the long-settled parts of the Bay State are greater than can be expected, for more than a generation at least, in newly settled regions.

We live in a climate and on a soil best adapted, from their very severity and sterility, to bring out the energies of mind and body, and to form a race of hardy and resolute men. We have our churches, our schools, our lyceums, our libraries, our intelligent and virtuous neighbors, and we wish our children should grow up under the influence of the institutions which our forefathers have formed and left to us, and which we have been endeavoring to improve.

CPSIA information can be obtained
at www.ICGtesting.com
Printed in the USA
BVHW041437220219
540923BV00007B/535/P

9 781397 315588